7 Strategi‹
Growth

To 'y...

TRANSFORM
WITHIN

*Thank you &
any truit & healing
has*

FAITH RUTO

*Begun! love
faith*

Transformwithin@faithruto.com

www.faithruto.com

www.transformation21st.com

I dedicate this book to my awesome family members (in the UK, Kenya and Uganda).

I love you all to the moon and forever!

I give thanks to GOD for blessing me and giving me FAITH!

To the loving memory and legacy of my grandmother – Consy Oming, "Mama Wa". Thank You!

PRAISE FOR "TRANSFORM WITHIN"

"Transform Within is an ambitious book, which covers a broad range of practical coaching strategies for professionals. It deals with seven strategies that are key to personal development, from discovering your own purpose to learning to let go and forgive.

It describes each strategy, illustrates the lessons learned from Faith's personal and clients' experience, and provides an excellent framework to take action.

As someone who has made the transition from the corporate into the entrepreneurial world, I found this book a very useful and practical guide to rediscover purpose and thrive in change.

Rather than being a theoretical academic book, this is firmly aimed at professionals and is essentially a collection of practical strategies and tools to inspire individuals to transform within. This is an excellent book for anyone looking to better their lives."

Dr Djamila Amimer, *CEO and Founder*
Mind Senses Global, the UK, www.mindsenses.com

———————————

Faith, thanks for sharing your personal stories. I think it's very authentic and genuine and will be very useful for many.

Melissa Kam, *Founder*, Gorendang.co.uk

"Transform Within is a fascinating book. If you are looking for transformational growth and Hope in your life, then you need to read this book. This book is for anyone who knows they have more in them, but needs guidance to unlock their true potential, discover and live their true purpose. Each chapter of the book challenges you to dare to dream bigger than you ever imagined."

Akwasi Frimpong, *Olympian, Ghana's first Skeleton Athlete, Motivational Speaker & Entrepreneur*

"As someone whose philosophy of life is to go-with-the-flow, I found Faith's book extremely inspiring. It has challenged me to examine my life and to determine whether I am living life to the fullest and making the most of the gifts I have been entrusted with. This is a very valuable and unexpected benefit, which I believe, was triggered by Faith's honesty and sincerity in sharing her struggles and her triumphs. I particularly endorse her exhortation to forgive those who have hurt us and to be part of a community."

Jonathan Pinto, *Associate Professor,* Organizational Behaviour and Negotiations at Imperial College Business School, the UK

"In the tumult of today's world, many people are searching for a greater sense of purpose. In her book, Faith writes with integrity as someone who has repeatedly faced her own fears,

transformed herself and is therefore able to offer authentic, practical advice. Her inspiring story provides guidance to others embarking on a transformation journey."

Susan Goldsworthy, *Co-author* of the award-winning books *Care to Dare* and *Choosing Change*.

"Wow! This is an awesome book! I love it and have learnt a lot. It's an easy-to-read book, very inspirational and transforma-tional. I learnt to re-evaluate myself and make a radical step to 'cultivate a growth mindset as opposed to a fixed mindset'. I like the way you end every chapter by causing the reader to reflect and come up with a "big idea" from the reading and make a self-evaluation."

Rev. Canon Dr. Johnson Ebong, *Author, Philanthropist, Founding Director* of Mentor College School and Karadali Development Limited, Uganda

---

"Wow! I always thought you were an amazing person but I didn't quite realise how much you have accomplished and what a role model you are. I would give your book five stars and I hope everyone else does too. It is clear, concise and can be read in one sitting, which a lot of books can't."

Rebecca, *Client Relations*, M&S

CONTENTS

Contents   9

Meet Faith   13

Getting started   23

Who should read this book?   27

How to use this book   29

Strategy 1: Discover your Purpose   **31**

Why you need to Discover your Purpose   33

How I found my Purpose   34

Massive Action for Purpose   41

Strategy 2: Choose Faith, not Fear   **43**

Why you need to choose Faith over Fear   45

How my clients overcame their fears   47

How I overcame my fears   51

Massive Action for Overcoming Fear   55

Strategy 3: Cultivate a Growth Mindset   **57**

Why you need to cultivate a Growth Mindset   59

How I use a Growth Mindset to help my clients   61

How I learned to cultivate a Growth Mindset   65

Massive Action for a Growth Mindset   67

Strategy 4: Develop Resilience   **69**

Why you need to Develop Resilience   71

How negative experiences can help us

Develop Resilience   74

Massive Action for Resilience   79

**Strategy 5: Create time for your Family
and Friends**   **81**

Why you need to find time for your Family

and Friends   83

How I have helped my clients make time

for Family and Friends   85

Massive Action for Family and Friends   89

Strategy 6: Be part of a Community   **91**

Why you need to be part of a Community   93

How I became part of a Community   96

Massive Action for Community   100

Strategy 7: Learn to Let Go and Forgive   **101**

Why you need to learn to Let Go and Forgive   103

How I learned to Let Go and Forgive   105

Massive Action for Forgiveness   110

Are you ready to change?   111

How to transform from within   115

Connect with Faith   119

Recommended reading   121

Acknowledgements   125

Endnotes   127

MEET FAITH

Photo by Ghatahora Photography

I am a mother, wife, founding director, certified coach and mentor. I empower my clients to thrive and succeed in their careers. In 2015, I set up a personal development consultancy Transformation21st Limited to help people thrive during personal and professional transformation. For more information about our services, please visit: **www.transformation21st.com.**

The company has grown organically and now supports clients in the UK and globally.

I often get asked the following questions:

- ✓ How did you discover your purpose to help people?

- ✓ How did you navigate your career during a time of constant change?

- ✓ How did you stay so positive during the adversities that you have faced in your life and career?

- ✓ How did you overcome your fear of public speaking?

- ✓ How do you help your clients become confident speakers?

- ✓ How do you cope with discrimination because of your race, faith or gender?

- ✓ How do you coach your clients to grow in their careers?

I am going to answer these questions here and throughout this book.

Let me start from the beginning. I was born in the north of Uganda, during the time of both Idi Amin's war and the Lord's Resistance civil war. Both my parents were young when I was born, so my mother's parents decided that they would look after me while my mother completed her nursing course. I lived with my grandparents until the age of 12. I arrived in London in the snowy and freezing cold winter of 1993. Shortly after my arrival, my mother took me to a secondary school. School life was different and difficult at times. I was a dedicated student and wanted to succeed despite being bullied and being predicted low grades. I left school with 11 GCSEs and went on to study 3 A levels at college and then a Bachelor of Science at a university. I graduated with a 2:1 in Business and Information Technology. So, as you can see, I didn't let other people's opinions or my circumstances define my potential.

My interest in self-help books and psychology really grew while I was at university. In the third year of my degree course, while working as an intern at British Airways, I also studied Psychology part-time at Middlesex College. I enjoyed learning about the connection between human emotions and behaviours. In my final year at university, I used visualisation techniques, such as writing down positive thoughts and my expected grades in colourful Post-it Notes, to stay motivated. My university friends thought I was crazy, but I had discovered the power of positive self-belief.

My career started as an IT graduate with Royal Dutch Shell in 2002. I was one of only three female professionals amongst a global team of 25. I wasn't treated any different to my male colleagues. I had excellent mentors within the team and my line managers were very supportive. After three years in IT, I wanted a more commercial role in Sales and Marketing, so I moved to Shell Marine where I managed and led change programmes across 20 countries. In 2007, I was promoted to a global change expert role across multiple business units. At the same time, I was actively involved with the company's diversity groups, which promoted gender and race equality. I also got married to my soul mate.

In 2008, shortly after the financial crisis, I made a bold decision to self-fund my Executive MBA (part-time) course at Imperial College Business School. I was nearly 30 years old. I felt, as a woman who wanted to have a career and children, embarking on my study before my 30th birthday was critical. I had to study for 30 hours a week whilst working full time. I loved everything about studying, especially the opportunity to study with a diverse group of professionals from different sectors and different countries. I enjoyed studying innovation, entrepreneurship, organisational behaviour and change management. In the second year of my course in 2009, I became pregnant with my first child.

Studying, working and being pregnant were a real challenge, but I believe that this episode of my life equipped me with resilience and determination to fulfil my potential.

I graduated in 2011 in the Royal Albert Hall, and months later I was shortlisted as an MBA Star at the prestigious Women of the Future Awards (WOF) held at the London Hilton hotel on Park Lane. At the WOF Awards, I met and spoke to Cherie Blair CBE (Cherie Booth Q.C.), the wife of the former UK Prime Minister, Tony Blair, and we discussed empowering women. It was there that I decided I wanted to mentor others, especially women. I am currently a volunteer mentor at the Cherie Blair Foundation for Women.

That evening, at the WOF Awards, I also had a conversation with the Shell Women's Network president. We discussed the challenges women returning from maternity leave face, and I proposed a retention strategy in the form of a maternity coaching programme for women going on and returning from maternity leave. I developed the concept for such a programme with a fellow colleague and the proposal was submitted to the sponsoring board. The board approved the programme and it was later rolled out across the organisation. I felt humbled that my concept had come to fruition and was now going to support many working women throughout the company.

In 2012, I had my second baby and took a year of maternity leave. Whilst on maternity leave, I was informed that due to restructuring, my role was at risk of redundancy. Having worked as a change consultant, I was very aware that the company was facing a time of continuous change. However, nothing could have prepared me for the emotional rollercoaster that followed. I felt angry, shocked, fearful and sad at the possibility of facing career uncertainty. It was during this time of uncertainty in my career that I realised that I didn't want to just chase money and career progression. I knew that the days of a "job for life" were now over. If I wanted to change career or find a role that suited my new life as a mother of two, I needed to go out and look for opportunities. I explored UK-based roles across different departments within Shell. I found a role in Shell Retail; the job was called Loyalty Innovator. I applied, went for the interview and was successful. I believe having an MBA played a key role in me getting that position. I enjoyed learning about customer journey experiences and working outside my comfort zone.

In 2014, I took a leap of faith decision to quit my corporate career to set up a personal development consultancy called Transformation21st

Limited. My mission is to help professionals and entrepreneurs grow and thrive during periods of change. I hope that this book will help people going through adversities and transitions in life and the workplace to emerge stronger. By writing this book, I hope that you will be empowered to transform from within and take massive actions to change your circumstances for the better.

GETTING STARTED

t's 5am on Friday 5th January 2019; everyone in my house is asleep except me. I have accomplished most of the personal and professional goals I set myself for 2018. I had:

✓ Delivered an empowering talk to over 200 staff from the Red Cross.

✓ Attended Tony Robbins' Unleash the Power Within 4-day conference in London and completed the famous hot-coal "Fire Walk" (temperature over 400 Celsius). I even have the t-shirt and a certificate signed by Tony Robbins!

✓ Lost 12 kg of weight in just 10 weeks. That is post-baby weight gained over 6 years gone in 10 weeks! This result was due to healthy eating, daily HIIT exercising at home, and running.

- ✓ Completed the Basingstoke Half Marathon in 2 hours 10 minutes.

- ✓ Kept a daily gratitude log and shared weekly Facebook postings called "TGIF".

- ✓ Secured a corporate contract to design and deliver a group coaching programme to help professionals build resilience to change for Shell.

- ✓ Travelled to Atlanta and saw the birthplace of one of my heroes – Dr Martin Luther King.

- ✓ Started learning to play golf and really enjoy it now.

- ✓ Enjoyed family vacation in the US.

But there was one thing I hadn't done: write this book. I struggled to put my thoughts down on paper.

I have now been awake for over 6 hours writing this book. I catch myself thinking "it's now or never" as I type each word. I decide to stay up all night and write this entire book in one sitting because I know that procrastination is the main reason I have not even made a start until now.

WHO SHOULD READ THIS BOOK?

This book is for you, if you want:

- ✓ to grow in your career

- ✓ to feel motivated and more fulfilled in your career and life

- ✓ to discover your purpose

- ✓ a smooth career transition

- ✓ to overcome your fear of public speaking

- ✓ to feel more confident

- ✓ to overcome burnout

- ✓ a better work-life balance

- ✓ inspiration to transform your career and life for the better

- ✓ to empower your employees to build resilience to change

Photo by Ezzidin Alwan

Don't forget to write down
your massive actions

HOW TO USE
THIS BOOK

This book will offer practical yet powerful ways to help you grow, find your purpose, live by faith and transform from within.

Each chapter is broken down into four sections, as follows:

- ✓ **Strategy** with a brief topic definition

- ✓ **Application** of each strategy using real-life stories (my clients' and my own)

- ✓ **A call for YOU to reflect** and come up with your own takeaway from each strategy

- ✓ **A call for YOU to take massive action**

Then, at the end of this book, I share different ways for you to connect with me and provide some resources and books for further reading.

You can start the book at any sequence. I suggest you complete the **reflection** and **massive action** tasks in each section before moving on to the next strategy to get the maximum value.

I also suggest you write down your **massive actions** and be clear on the outcome you want to see. If you commit to each strategy like my clients and I have, you will experience growth and resilience in your professional and personal life.

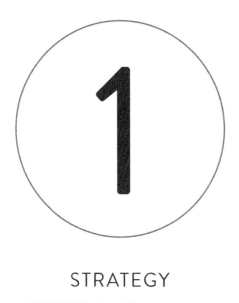

STRATEGY

DISCOVER YOUR PURPOSE

Photo by Ezzidin Alwan

Faith living out her purpose as an international speaker and coach

WHY YOU NEED TO
DISCOVER YOUR PURPOSE

Purpose is defined as: "why you do something or why something exists".[1] Without a deeper understanding of your own purpose or what drives you in your career and life, you will simply exist instead of thriving. You will not feel fulfilled in your career and life. Without knowing your purpose, you will lack resilience when faced with adversities in your career. Knowing your purpose is the starting point to fulfilling your true potential. Knowing your purpose guides your decisions and propels you forward.

HOW I FOUND
MY PURPOSE

n 2014, I was in my early 30s when I found myself asking, "Why am I here?" and "Is there another calling for me?" I had achieved most of the professional and personal goals that I had set myself when I was 18 years old.

For example:

✓   I had graduated with a 2:1

✓   I had worked for an international organisation

✓   I had travelled to over 30 countries

✓   I had completed an Executive MBA

✓   I got married before age 30

- ✓ I became a homeowner at 25 years old

- ✓ I was a committed Christian, supportive friend and close to my family

- ✓ I had mentored students from disadvantaged backgrounds

Yet, despite achieving all this and more, I felt I was missing something. I was unfulfilled and felt there must be more that I was meant to be doing. Perhaps you can relate to my emotions. What I was missing was purpose. I needed a more compelling reason to go to work other than making money. I needed to know that, should my life come to an end, I had left a legacy of some sort. I realised that I wanted to make a positive impact on the lives of many people.

As a Christian, I prayed for God to reveal to me what my purpose was. I had read many books on how to find your purpose but none helped me, as most of the books suggested looking externally.

Although many people seek their purpose outside of themselves, I have long believed that our purpose is inside us. It's hidden inside our interests, talents and gifts. For me, I had always loved helping people. I am not sure where I got my desire to help people. On reflection, I often wondered whether I got it from my grandmother, Consy Oming, who raised me from the age of 1 to 12. Or from my mother (Rosette) who has worked for the NHS for the last 30 years as a senior radiographer.

I grew up in the north of Uganda, in a small village called Ngai, where we didn't have much in terms of material belongings. I shared a small bedroom with my cousin, Eunice. I owned two pairs of shoes – one for church and one for school. We didn't have much (e.g. no electricity, no TV, no car). If we wanted water, we fetched it from the well. If we ran out of firewood for cooking, my cousins and I went out and collected wood from the nearby bushes.

Over the years, I have returned to
Uganda and I am always amazed at
how content my relatives are compared
to many of us who have so much.
Discovering your purpose
now is important for your mental
and emotional well-being.

But I grew up seeing my family share what little they had with everyone. I felt loved and encouraged to be the best I could be from a young age. Being a part of a community where everyone played their significant role showed me that when you live a purpose-driven life, you feel fulfilled.

Over the years I have returned to Uganda, I am always amazed at how content my relatives are compared to many of us who have so much. Discovering your purpose now is important for your mental and emotional well-being.

My desire to help others was ingrained in me from an early age. So, going back to that winter evening in February 2014 when I found myself asking, "What is my calling in life?" I got a clear and loud answer: "Why don't you quit your job?"

At first, I thought it was my husband suggesting I quit my job and become a stay-at-home mum. But when I turned around, I realised that there was no one there. I was getting an intuition that I needed to face my fear! At the time, I felt God was speaking to me. I heard the voice again, "Quit and walk by faith." I knew immediately that I had to resign from my corporate job. The next day, I drove to work with complete peace of mind; I took a risk and left my corporate career for an adventure to empower other people to thrive. Now, I enjoy coaching professionals and entrepreneurs to discover their purpose, build resilience and increase their self-confidence. I am living my purpose now by doing a job that I love and find very rewarding.

REFLECTION

WHAT ARE YOUR
KEY TAKEAWAYS?

A.

B.

Massive Action
for Purpose

(1) Have you ever thought about your purpose?

(2) Take a moment now to do the following tasks:

   a.   Make a list of WHY you are in your current career

   b.   Make a list of what motivates you in your job

   c.   Make a list of your passions

   d.   Make a list of what you enjoy doing

(3) Look at your lists, are you pursuing your purpose NOW?

(4) Go online and research ways to discover your purpose.

(5) Try and set aside quiet time to meditate or pray on a regular basis. When we are quiet and away from distractions, we can tune in to what our heart and gut are telling us.

STRATEGY

CHOOSE FAITH, NOT FEAR

Faith overcoming her fear of heights at the
Great Wall of China, Beijing

WHY YOU NEED TO
CHOOSE FAITH OVER FEAR

Faith is defined as "having great trust or confidence in something or someone".[2] You need to have trust in your abilities and trust your gut instincts when facing change in your career and life. It is important to have self-confidence and self-esteem to grow in your professional life. Having faith is about having hope and being optimistic when facing adversities and challenges. It is about trusting that everything will work out fine. It is also about investing your energy, time and resources to ensure that things do turn out positively.

I know I am living by faith when I feel I can move mountains. But when I am fearful, I feel afraid to fail, I feel indecisive, frustrated, alone and unable to move forward.

Whether your faith lies in God or in yourself, make a choice today to live your life by faith, not fear. FEAR is not real. In fact, it is often said that FEAR stands for "False Evidence Appearing Real." (Source: www.psychologytoday.com)

HOW MY CLIENTS
OVERCAME THEIR FEARS

S ometimes, fear can cause us to miss great opportunities in our life or career. Since becoming a coach, I have met and worked with many highly intelligent clients who live their life by fear. For example, a client who was frustrated by their job was too scared to voice their feelings to their line manager because they feared they might get fired. Another client was due a promotion, but the time came and passed. After two years of feeling frustrated and undervalued by their employer, they were ready to quit. After working with me, they realised that fear was holding them back. They summoned the courage and spoke to their manager. They were promoted to a Director position within weeks.

66

*I know I am living by faith when I feel
I can move mountains. But when I
am fearful, I feel afraid to fail, I feel
indecisive, frustrated, alone and unable
to move forward.*

99

Another client was implementing change in their organisation; they wanted me to run a workshop on resilience but were afraid that the staff would not be engaged. The opposite happened. After the workshop, all the employees who attended felt that their employer really valued them and this, in return, empowered the staff to view the reorganisation as an opportunity rather than a threat.

A recent client approached me because he had a fear of public speaking. His fear stemmed from an early presenting experience at university where other students had laughed at him. The experience scared him and lowered his self-esteem. He was now a very senior director but still had this massive fear of public speaking. I coached him over many weeks. I encouraged him to think, "What is the worst that can happen when I next present?". I encouraged him to practice and to watch other people presenting. He identified speakers that he liked and practised. After 3 months of coaching and practising, he secured a major business deal. He was able to do something that, months earlier, he wouldn't have thought possible – deliver a near perfect presentation in front of clients. He overcame his fear by prac-tising, by gaining self-confidence and by having faith that all would go well. Our attitude impacts our behaviour and our results.

To overcome your fear, you need to put in the work and have a positive mindset.

HOW I OVERCAME
MY FEARS

Like many of my clients, I used to have a massive fear of public speaking. According to the UK magazine *Psychologies,* the fear of public speaking is greater in most people than the fear of death. In fact, when I give seminars on public speaking, people often say to me, "You are brave, I'd rather die than give a speech."

15 years ago, I was one of those people. If I had to speak up in meetings at work, I would shake and murmur words. But one day, I decided that I had to put aside my fear of being judged. Encouraged by my coach, Sonia, I joined the speaking organisation, Toastmaster, at London Business School. It was one of the best decisions of my career. By

making time to practice speaking in front of a live audience, I was able to let go of my fears and gain the confidence to speak in public.

For many years, I was afraid of heights. In 2010, while I was studying for an Executive MBA, I went on a study tour to China (Beijing and Shanghai). At the time, I was also four months pregnant with my first child. With the excitement of walking on one of the eight wonders of the world – the Great Wall of China – I forgot that I was scared of heights. In fact, I seemed to have forgotten this fear until it was too late. As soon as I climbed up those stairs and looked down, I realised that I couldn't move. In fact, I completely froze. I was overcome by fear. My internal fear stories bubbled up: "What if I fall? What if…!" After 10 minutes of self-doubting and debating, I choose to close my eyes and hold on tight to one of my fellow student's hands, Dr Ali. I placed my trust in him and took baby steps forward, one at a time. I was relieved when I got to the top. From that day, I chose to walk by faith, not sight. Sometimes, we have to face our deepest fears in order to move forward. As this story shows, I couldn't have done it alone; we need to reach out to our support network.

Over the years, I have conquered many of my fears, for example, my fear of drowning. I taught myself how to swim by watching my children's swimming lessons. Once I was more confident in water, I took swimming lessons to perfect my techniques. Since then, I have learnt how to surf. A few years ago, I went to Croatia for a short holiday, and we took a catamaran boat out to sea. I felt brave enough to jump out and swim in the sea. When you overcome your fears, it is the best feeling in the world! It is true freedom because you are no longer held back from going forward. Don't let fear of anything hold you back in your career or life.

REFLECTION

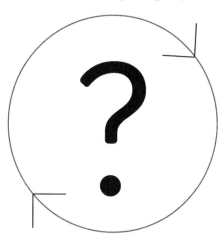

WHAT ARE YOUR
KEY TAKEAWAYS?

A. B.

Massive Action
for Overcoming Fear

(1) Are you living your life by faith or by fear?

(2) Make a list of all the fears that are holding you back in your career or life, e.g. fear of networking, fear of public speaking.

(3) What opportunities are you passing on by not facing your fears?

(4) Make a list of actions that you will take today to start overcoming your fears.

(5) Identify resources, e.g. books, mentors and experts, that can help you overcome your fears.

STRATEGY

CULTIVATE A GROWTH MINDSET

Faith took this photograph in Padstow, Cornwall, the UK, after a stormy afternoon. When you are a facing your own storm in life, remember the rainbow, don't give up

WHY YOU NEED TO
CULTIVATE A
GROWTH MINDSET

Physiologist Professor Carol Dweck is famous for her research into what is now known as a Fixed Mindset and a Growth Mindset. Professor Carol Dweck explained that when you are using a growth mindset, you believe that you are in control of your ability. For example, you have a belief that you can learn and improve your skills. Having a growth mindset is very important for people who want to take more risks and step outside their comfort zone. Your mindset will determine how you handle failures, success, rejection, criticism and change. To grow and transform in your career, you need to be willing to persevere when faced with challenges and setbacks.

Having a growth mindset will equip you with the capacity to deal with challenges better than when you have a fixed mindset. A person with a fixed mindset may believe that their abilities and intelligence determine everything. When they fail, they will blame themselves. There is a difference between taking responsibility for your own actions and overstating your ability to determine everything. A fixed mindset person will take longer to recover from setbacks and negative feedback.

According to Professor Carol Dweck, we bounce between these two mindsets. Most of the time we don't even notice it. It also becomes important when we start to believe the limitations and lies that we are telling ourselves.

HOW I USE A GROWTH MINDSET
TO HELP MY CLIENTS

I n my coaching practice, I have worked with many clients who feel stuck in their career. They feel stuck because they perceive their career outcome as a direct result of their efforts and hard work. They fear stepping outside their comfort zone because of uncertainties and the fear of failure. Through coaching, I am able to demonstrate to my clients that simply staying stuck is not a sustainable option that would make them happy.

Through simple steps, clients analyse failure as an opportunity to develop and improve. They are able to transform from being self-critical to asking the right questions. For example, "What can I learn from this experience?" and "What can

I do differently next time?" Many professionals that I have worked with usually fear the end-of-year performance review because any negative feedback usually contradicts any positive feedback. According to Professor Carol Dweck, we can cultivate a growth mindset by changing our language. For example, instead of saying, "I am rubbish at public speaking," say instead, "I am not yet an expert at public speaking." Just by using the word "yet" we are opening our mind up for opportunities and possibilities.

HOW I LEARNED TO CULTIVATE
A GROWTH MINDSET

A person with a growth mindset is likely to handle negative feedback better than a person with a fixed mindset. I used to believe that my failures were due to me not being "good enough" or "intelligent enough." I realised that I needed to learn to move on from this negative feedback. I also learnt to embrace new opportunities with curiosity.

Having a growth mindset will help you to embrace change instead of fearing it. You will be able to ask for support from others when you need it. When you have a growth mindset, you are resilient and not defined by your circumstances.

Having a growth mindset will help you to embrace change instead of fearing it. You will be able to ask for support from others when you need it. When you have a growth mindset, you are resilient and not defined by your circumstances.

Transforming your mindset means letting go of what other people think of you. It's time to stop worrying and start living. It's about letting go of your own self-limiting beliefs and behaviours. To transform within, you will need a growth mindset.

Yes, we are living in a VUCA time! VUCA is not another tropical disease, it stands for: Volatile, Uncertain, Complex and Ambiguous. The truth is that no one can really predict the future anymore. Our power lies in using our brains and eliminating negative self-beliefs.

We cannot apply the old principles to our lives or careers and expect to get the same results. We need to adjust our mindsets and leadership styles.

Our organisations need professionals and leaders who are more flexible, agile and ambidextrous. Cultivating a growth mindset is good for you and also for people around you.

REFLECTION

WHAT ARE YOUR
KEY TAKEAWAYS?

A.

B.

Massive Action
for a Growth Mindset

1. Would you say you have a growth mindset or a fixed mindset?

2. Reflect back to your past failures, were you using your growth mindset or a fixed mindset?

3. Make a list of your current challenges or shortcomings (e.g. lack of confidence).

4. Reword your list in action 3 above, inserting the word "yet". For example, if you wrote, "I lack confidence," write "I don't have confidence yet." Notice how powerful adding "yet" is.

(5) What opportunities have you been putting off because of your fixed mindset? E.g. I am not an expert in that area, so I won't apply for that job. What if you said, "I want to learn to become an expert, so I will acquire the necessary skills."

STRATEGY

DEVELOP
RESILIENCE

WHY YOU NEED TO
DEVELOP RESILIENCE

R esilience is defined as our ability to bounce back after a setback. It's our attitude, self-efficacy and behaviours that determine our resilience. Resilience can be developed over time.

The German philosopher, Friedrich Nietzsche, said, "That which does not kill us, makes us stronger." Or you may have heard the pop song by Kelly Clarkson, "what doesn't kill you makes you stronger".[3]

Resilience is important for career success. We no longer have a job for life. Being resilient to constant changes in the workplace is the key to thriving during change. Being resilient will enable you to adapt and grow in your career.

A person who has resilience embraces change as an opportunity. That person has a growth mindset and is able to learn from failures and move forward. This is a skill that is important for innovation and personal growth.

Not all changes are bad, some changes are positive; meanwhile, other changes can be painful. For example, a person who is not ready for redundancy will handle the experience completely differently to a person who is expecting redundancy.

The key to living a successful life is no longer about working harder but instead being resilient to change in our personal and professional lives. None of us is immune to the knocks of life, the things that go wrong, or the people that let us down. We can't live a life without these shadows but what we can do is change the way we react to them. This is important as we grow stronger in our skills, abilities, leadership and self-confidence.

Resilience is important for career success. We no longer have a job for life. Being resilient to constant changes in the workplace is the key to thriving during change. Being resilient will enable you to adapt and grow in your career.

HOW NEGATIVE EXPERIENCES
CAN HELP US
DEVELOP RESILIENCE

I n October 2018, I was invited to exhibit and deliver a keynote speech at one of Europe's biggest business shows at ExCeL London. Preparing for the event took hours and a large financial investment. Over 30,000 people attended the conference, because the event was well promoted.

It was during the run-up to this event on November 5th that my life's perspective and focus changed. On my way to the conference centre for the preparations, I was involved in a car accident in London. Out of nowhere, a white van pulled up onto my lane at high speed and narrowly missed hitting me directly. I literally saw my life flash before my eyes. Luckily, I slammed on the brakes. I was in complete shock and very distraught. To make matters worse, the other driver came out of their van shouting and yelling abuse at me. In my 20 years of driving around the UK, I had never been involved in a car accident. Thank God no one was hurt. Luckily, I was less than 2 miles from the London ExCeL Centre. Despite feeling shaken and scared to drive on, I proceeded with my preparations for the show. I made a conscious decision that I had to go ahead with the show preparation. I also remembered to be grateful that the worse had not happened.

On the same day, a few hours later, I returned to collect my daughter from horse-riding school. I was immediately informed that she had fallen off a horse but was fine and had got up straight away and got back on the horse. I recall thinking, "this is what resilience means." In life, we sometimes fall down, but we must get up.

However, a few hours later when we were at home, my daughter complained of headache, nausea and head soreness. We were taken to the hospital in an ambulance. We waited for over 5 hours to be seen. After an examination, the doctor confirmed that my daughter had concussion and a whiplash injury on her left shoulder. I thanked God that she was okay, as it could have been worse.

It was at 3am the night before the show that self-doubt crept in. My daughter had to stay at home now; I needed to find emergency childcare for her for at least the next two days while I was at the London ExCeL business show. My husband was away travelling for work and I had no relatives nearby that could look after her. Most working parents know the emotions involved in frantically trying to find last-minute childcare. I was also conflicted by my decision – should I still go ahead with the business show? I felt like giving up on going to the show; I was emotionally tired and drained. But thanks to my supportive friends (Joy, Raquel, Varsha and Neena) and my mum, I was able to continue with the show, where I delivered one of my best talks on resilience.

I am glad that I didn't give up despite all the obstacles that I faced leading up to this event. A showreel video was produced and can be viewed on the following link: https://youtu.be/3YSjYTm-dxdo (Video credits to Nicholas Velasco)

Throughout my professional and personal life, I have faced many adversities. Each time I have found the will to continue. I have built my resilience by surrounding myself with positive friends, families, consuming content that helps me grow, and relying on my faith in God. I also find exercising, especially running, really helps me to refocus and feel positive.

REFLECTION

WHAT ARE YOUR
KEY TAKEAWAYS?

A.   B.

Massive Action
for Resilience

(1) On a scale of 0 to 10 (0 being no resilience, 10 being very resilient) how would you rate your resilience to facing challenges in the workplace and life?

(2) If you scored less than 5, what do you need to do to increase your resilience?

(3) If you scored higher than a 7, make a list of strategies that have helped you become more resilient. For example, practising mindfulness, exercising, and so on.

(4) Can you think of a situation in your career or life when you had to turn a negative experience into a positive experience/opportunity?

(5) What other actions do you need to take to increase your resilience? For example, make time for friends and family, take some "me time".

STRATEGY

CREATE TIME FOR YOUR FAMILY AND FRIENDS

WHY YOU NEED TO FIND TIME
FOR YOUR FAMILY
AND FRIENDS

You have probably read or heard about studies on the top five life regrets of the dying by Bronnie Ware.[4] Unsurprisingly, spending more time with family and friends is amongst the top five. No one mentioned working harder, yet this is what most of us do instead of spending real quality time with our loved ones. More of us are feeling lonely, depressed and disconnected because we are not spending enough time with our families. These are challenges that my clients and I face as a result of work and self-imposed busyness.

In many cultures, it is the norm to sit down and share a meal every day with your family. But with our super-paced busy lives, we rarely make time to share a meal or spend much time with each other anymore. Some of us are living distances away from our families and friends. Although technology has enabled us to stay in touch, we are lacking physical closeness.

A loving friendship and families are the key to emotional well-being and resilience. It is not easy to find time to balance family life and work for many professionals and entrepreneurs.

HOW I HAVE HELPED MY CLIENTS
CREATE TIME FOR FAMILY AND FRIENDS

There are no right or wrong formulae to achieve the ultimate balance. From my own experience, I believe we all need to define what balance looks like for ourselves. Once you know what balance feels like for you and your family and friends, you then need to create time. Don't make excuses or become complacent.

Time is the only commodity that we cannot buy back.

I would like to think that I have always made time for my family and friends. I make it my highest priority to put my family first. However, there are

A loving friendship and families are the key to emotional well-being and resilience. It is not easy to find time to balance family life and work for many professionals and entrepreneurs.

busy times when you have urgent deadlines. For example, there were times when I would rush bedtime stories because I needed to log back onto my laptop to complete work or send emails on weekends or even during family holiday times. One-offs are okay, but when working without boundaries becomes a habit, you can easily lose touch with your immediate family.

Over the years, I have coached executives on how to carve out time for family and friends. A client approached me because they were working 14 hours a day and hardly saw their young family. My client felt she needed to make a change, as her work pattern was adversely affecting her health, her marriage and the relationship she had with her children.

REFLECTION

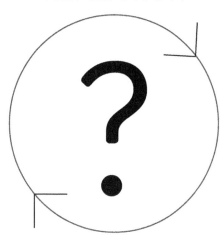

WHAT ARE YOUR
KEY TAKEAWAYS?

A.

Massive Action for Family and Friends

B.

1. Are you satisfied with the quantity and quality of time that you are currently spending with your family and friends? If no, why not?

2. What is getting in the way of you spending more quality time with your family and friends?

3. What actions can you take today to increase the quantity and quality of the time you spend with your family and friends?

(4) What steps will you take to achieve your desired balance?

(5) If you are happy with your quantity and quality of time with family and friends, ask your family and friends if they are happy. It is important to get regular feedback to ensure everyone is happy.

STRATEGY

BE PART OF A COMMUNITY

WHY YOU NEED TO
BE PART OF A COMMUNITY

Your community is the company you keep. Whether physical friends or those influencers you follow online, your community can be a source of support and inspiration. I have read many books by psychologists on how to achieve success and happiness. Being part of a community is very important for personal well-being, growth and resilience. Studies of mental well-being have shown that loneliness is a major issue for professionals. Being a part of a community can help with mental well-being.

There is an African proverb that says, "If you want to go fast, go alone. If you want to go far, go together."

I have seen both the advantages and disadvantages of technology when it comes to helping professionals be a part of a community. We need to have a balance between building our community solely online and offline. Human contact is still very important for us to feel like we're a part of a community. I have noticed that as we grow older, our circle of friends may decrease. Busyness of life may get in the way of us participating in activities that make us a part of community. For example, when we work longer hours or when we move away from where we have grown up, we can lose our sense of community.

66

There is an African proverb that says,
"If you want to go fast, go alone. If you
want to go far, go together."

99

HOW I BECAME
PART OF A COMMUNITY

Throughout my professional life, I have made it my mission to be a part of a community. I achieved this by joining various interest groups with a purpose that resonated with my values. I was, for example, a member of Women's Network, Christian Network, BAME network and various online groups. I have always had a mentor and a coach for guidance and advice. Outside work, I am an active community member in my local church and my children's school. I actively join local business networking groups where I can share my knowledge and also learn from others.

If you are going through a change in your career or life, make sure you surround your-

self with positive like-minded people who will build you up and encourage you to grow.

Be mindful about how much time you invest in building a community. There were times when I was so busy building a career that I didn't make time to be a part of a community. You will realise this when you suddenly find yourself alone with no real support system. This can also happen when you become a parent. After I had my second child we relocated away from London. I stopped working. Suddenly, I found myself without a community. It felt lonely. You may identify with some of what I went through.

Don't make the same mistake that I did by being too busy; create time for forming and nurturing your community. I reclaimed my community by becoming a part of a cause that had shared values to me. For example, I volunteered to be a public speaker ambassador for a gynaecological cancer charity called Eve Appeal Charity. I created a Facebook page and started sharing information on how women could get early diagnosis for cancers and also provided information on how women could get support. I also ran coffee mornings at my house where I invited my new neighbours and mums from schools. Slowly, I felt I had a community online and offline.

Although I enjoy being part of a business community, I couldn't attend my local business networking events. Most were run early at 6.30am or late in the evenings. As a working mum who wants to drop her kids to school and do the school pickups, I struggled to attend these networking events. So in 2017, I decided to launch my own lunchtime networking group. Over the years, I have formed and developed a close-knit community of like-minded business entrepreneurs.

REFLECTION

WHAT ARE YOUR
KEY TAKEAWAYS?

Massive Action
for Community

(1) Do you feel that you are part of a
community?

(2) Can you identify communities that you
are part of today?

(3) What values are you getting from being
a part of a community?

(4) What values are you contributing to your
community?

(5) What is stopping you from being a part of
a community?

STRATEGY

LEARN TO LET GO AND FORGIVE

The last photograph I took with my grandma under a mango tree in Lira Uganda, before she passed away in 2008

WHY YOU NEED TO LEARN TO
LET GO AND FORGIVE

Throughout our careers and lives, we are going to face situations and people who will make us feel angry, upset and disappointed. The easiest option is to hold blame and anger. However, this is unhealthy and counterproductive. It is very important to learn the power of letting go and forgiveness if we want to grow and transform from within. The ability to let go and forgive is, of course, not easy, but it is important because it enables us to open ourselves to possibilities and growth.

It is important to let go because if we don't, we are living in the past. If we don't forgive, we are focusing on the past, not the present moment. Letting go and forgiving takes more energy than holding a grudge or anger. Letting go and forgiveness is not about forgetting. It is a slow process of acknowledging that what has happened has happened. It cannot be changed. To let go and to forgive is a choice you make. The first step to learning to let go and forgive is communication. It is important to share with the people that have caused you anger how their behaviours and actions have made you feel. The next step is then you making a decision that you will let go and forgive. Often, the people who have upset you may not even be aware that they have wronged you.

Instead of feeling angry and frustrated, have the courage to let go. You will actually be doing yourself a favour. You will open up opportunities and feel happier and lighter.

HOW I LEARNED TO
LET GO AND FORGIVE

Like many of you, I have had situations both in my personal and professional life that have not been easy to forgive or let go of, but I have pushed myself to let go and forgive because I felt I needed to live in the present, not the past. I have achieved nothing by playing a victim or shifting blame on to others for the way that I felt.

The worst example from my professional life came shortly after my second baby, when I went back into my office for a "keep in touch day". My son was only two months old. My then boss and HR representative thought that this day would be a good time to issue me with a possible notice of redundancy. I was handed an envelope with a letter

"

Instead of feeling angry and frustrated, have the courage to let go. You will actually be doing yourself a favour. You will open up opportunities and feel happier and lighter.

"

stating that my role was at risk of redundancy. I was in shock. I felt angry with the company, my boss and HR for essentially ruining my maternity leave. Instead of enjoying my maternity leave, I spent days and nights worrying about my career and future. After six months of feeling like a victim, I realised I had to forgive and move on. Years later, I discovered that it is not uncommon for companies to make returning mums redundant following maternity leave. If you are faced with a similar situation, try to forgive, as otherwise you will be holding yourself back. Had I not gone through this experience, I would not have had the courage to explore other roles and even start up my own business.

In my personal life, I grew up without knowing my father due to the civil war in Uganda and also because my parents were of different religious backgrounds and very young. They didn't stay together. For many years, I felt very upset and angry with my parents for not being in my life when I was growing up. But as I grew older and understood why they were unable to be with me, I was faced with a choice – to remain angry or to forgive? Forgiveness took many years. In 2016, after nearly 25 years of lost contact with my biological father, we reunited, and I realised that choosing to forgive was the best decision ever. It allowed us space to create a new relationship.

REFLECTION

WHAT ARE YOUR KEY TAKEAWAYS?

A. B.

Massive Action
for Forgiveness

(1) Do you need to forgive and let go of anything? It can be a person or a situation in the past.

(2) Who do you need to forgive in your life or career today in order to move forward?

(3) In what ways are your decisions today shaped by past hurt?

(4) What opportunities are you missing by staying angry?

(5) What support do you need to forgive and let go?

ARE YOU READY TO CHANGE?

don't want to scare you, but after seeing loved ones die, I have come to a realisation that our time here on Earth is limited. We must live with a purpose to serve and make a difference. When you go to work day in day out, create time to pause and reflect – what do you want your legacy to be? What do you want to be remembered for? What do you want to live for?

I hope you will create time to take massive actions to transform from within.

Make a decision, from this moment on; don't put off what you can do today until tomorrow or later. To achieve your purpose and big goals, you need to TRANSFORM NOW. Don't wish you had a better life or a better opportunity. You need to take ownership of your decisions and behaviours today. Make a decision to live your life by FAITH and not FEAR.

Suzanne D. Williams: Unsplash

Embrace change!
Realise your full potential!

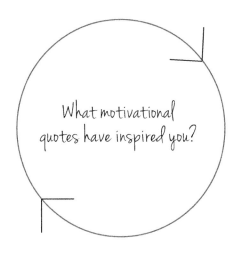

What motivational
quotes have inspired you?

HOW TO TRANSFORM FROM WITHIN

✓ Put into practice each of the 7 strategies that you have read in this book.

✓ Complete each massive action.

✓ Join our community by signing up for regular motivational content from Faith: **www.transformation21st.com**

✓ Book your FREE coaching strategy call with Faith.

✓ Book Faith to speak at your next corporate event: **info@transformation21st.com**

✓ Make a decision TODAY to start living by FAITH rather than Fear!

Faith and her team can support you with:

- ✓ increasing your self-confidence

- ✓ increasing public speaking confidence

- ✓ delivering keynote speeches

- ✓ delivering motivational talks

- ✓ career coaching

- ✓ life coaching

- ✓ building resilience

- ✓ embracing organisational changes in the workplace

- ✓ overcoming limiting self-beliefs

- ✓ considering further studies such as an MBA

...and more

Photo by Alex

Faith visiting her first primary school in Ngai, north of Uganda in 2001. Don't let your past determine your present and future successes.

CONNECT WITH FAITH
ON SOCIAL MEDIA
AND LEAVE A BOOK REVIEW

I would love to hear feedback on how this book has transformed your thinking, your career or life. Share your review on Amazon, feedback on social media and don't forget to tag @faithrutot21st. This will help other professionals grow in their journey to career and life fulfilment.

Transformwithin@faithruto.com

www.FaithRuto.com, www.transformation21st.com

www.facebook.com/TransformWithBook

www.instagram.com/faithrutoT21st

www.linkedin.com/in/faithrutoT21st

@faithrutoT21st

RECOMMENDED READING

O ver the last 20 years, my interest and passion for personal development has led me to read the books listed below. In their own way, they have positively influenced my thoughts, mindset and behaviours. I hope you can build on your knowledge from this book by reading and following these authors.

Purpose, Passion and Faith

Awaken The Giant Within by Tony Robbins

Becoming by Michelle Obama

Conversations with God by Neale Donald Walsch

Dreams from My Father by Barack Obama

Fearless Passion by Yong Kang Chan

The Audacity of Hope by Barack Obama

Purpose by Jessica Huie

The Bible – New International Version

The Busy Christian's Guide to Busyness by Tim Chester

Forgiveness, Mindset and Resilience

Conquering Storms of Life by Rev. Canon Dr. Johnson Ebong

Conversations with Myself by Nelson Mandela

Letter to My Daughter by Maya Angelou

Mindset: The New Psychology of Success by Professor Carol Dweck

The Chimp Paradox by Professor Steve Peters

Career, Change and Work-Life Balance

AdaptAbility by M.J Ryan

Choosing Change by Walter McFarland and Susan Goldsworthy

Eat That Frog by Brian Tracy

Escape the Cubicle by Sukhi Jutla

How To Be Really Productive by Grace Marshall

Lean In by Sheryl Sandberg

Make Change Work for You by Scott Steinberg

Thrive by Arianna Huffington

Start Up and Entrepreneurship

It Started with a Pound by Matthew Larcome

Self Made by Bianca Miller-Cole and Byron Cole

The Lean Startup by Eric Ries

ACKNOWLEDGEMENTS

To all my clients, thank you for being my inspiration and encouraging me to write this book.

I am grateful to the following people for their direct or indirect help in my writing of this book. My family, Dr Anthony Ruto, Isha Cole, Melissa Kam (Founder, www.Gorendang.co.uk), Varsha Amin (CEO, www.LotusX.co.uk), Rev. Canon Dr. Johnson Ebong and Amanda Alexander PCC (Multi-Award-Winning Coach).

Editing, Formatting and Cover Design: I AM Self-Publishing www.iamselfpublishing.com

To YOU the reader, thank you for choosing to read this book.

ENDNOTES

1. Dictionary.cambridge.org

2. Cambridge Dictionary

3. https://youtube/Xn676-fLq7I

4. *The Top Five Regrets of the Dying: A Life Transformed by the Dearly Departing* by Bronnie Ware

Printed in Great Britain
by Amazon